Improving Chances

Chances

The Story of the Good Shepherd Special
School, Uganda

ISBN 978-1-291-35442-3

Acknowledgements

Thankyou to Asumpta and her mother, and to Simon and his mother, for allowing me to use their stories and their pictures. Names and details of other chidren have been changed.

This little book is dedicated to

Peter Mount CBE, and the Trustees of "Helping Uganda Schools",

the Rev Maama Goretti Kabakaala, former Mother General of the Banyatereza Sisters,

and the late Rev Fr Albert Byaruhanga,

without whom The Good Shepherd School might never

have been,

and to good Samaritans Marian and Pawlik.

It was written in memory of

Sister Maureen Farrell FCJ

whose wisdom and compassion made all she met the richer.

"Improving Chances" is sold in aid of "Improving Chances for Ugandans,"

a UK registered charity which also supports the Good Shepherd School.

Author's note:

In the late 1940's, as a very small child, I spent several years with my parents in Uganda. Initially we were in Masaka, and later Fort Portal , where my father, who had been a Family Doctor in the UK, first taught basic health care skills to the local population, and then acted as District Medical Officer. Although I remember little of this experience, except the Swahili for "Come here...quickly!", I was always fascinated by the stories my parents told of their time in Africa, and I felt drawn to return. It was not until I retired, however, that I found the time to do so.

In the meantime, I myself trained as a doctor, and spent most of my working life in paediatrics, developing a special interest in the care of children with long term conditions and disability. My first paediatric post was at Queen Mary's Hospital, Carshalton, when this was still a long stay hospital for children with disabilities, as well as providing acute services. Much early work on the education of children with learning difficulties was done here, and the experience I gained there has stayed with me, and inspired me, throughout my career. Latterly, I was Consultant Paediatrician with a special interest in neurodisability in Bolton, from where I retired in 2007.

In early 2008, having learnt of her project through mutual friends, I travelled to Fort Portal to work with Sr Theresa Abigaba for three months as she began her journey into special needs education in Uganda, and since then I have returned annually, on two occasions with my daughters who have each also made a professional contribution to the development of the Good Shepherd School . I have been privileged over this time to observe the growth of a very special project and the establishment of a school that is an inspiration to all in concept and design.

And I am not the only one to be in thrall to the school: Sr Theresa and her children have touched many hearts ,too many to mention individually, but they include Rev Alison Hardy and the congregation of All Saints Church, Stand; Rev Monsignor John Allen and the congregation of Our Lady of Grace, Prestwich; and good friends, Rev Sr

Lydia, Rita, and Fr Pat Tansey. I would also like to pause here to remember with love those others , as well as Sr Maureen and Fr Albert, who have died and left us but whose names will always be associated with the Good Shepherd School: Janet Crook, Dr Aurea, Derrick Scampion, and Angus Hindley.

Patricia Scampion

February 2013

Prologue

"Disability is not Inability"

It is a December day in 2009, eighty children are gathered on a hill on the outskirts of Fort Portal in Western Uganda. With them are some of their parents, their teachers, a good number of Sisters from the nearby Virika Convent, a smattering of local dignitaries, a few white visitors, and the curious from the neighbourhood. Here, among the foothills of the Rwenzori mountains (the "Mountains of the Moon"), beneath the equatorial sun, a crowd is growing...and waiting. The children try to suppress their excitement: this is all new for them. They fidget, they hop from one foot to the other, they try not to crumple the posters they've made with their teachers in school: "Disability is not Inability", and "Every Child has a Right to Education". They are about to march through the centre of Fort Portal, and, though they don't know it, they are the realisation of a dream, the dream of the day's organiser, Sister Theresa Abigaba.

Today, though, Sister has no time for dreaming! At the edge of the group, in her dove grey habit and her stout shoes, she is talking rapidly into her mobile phone, as the English guests look surreptitiously at their watches and smile bravely at "Uganda time". The band has not arrived and without it the march will surely lose some of its spectacle. The instruments have been locked away for safe keeping, and someone has gone missing with the keys! An hour passes. It rains briefly. "Local" drums are sent for... they, at least, will liven things up. Then, just as the decision is made to start off without them, the band arrive: rapidly donning their uniforms and toting their instruments. The parade can begin.

The children are from the Good Shepherd School... the school Sr Theresa built and opened in 2008 with the help of a UK based charity, "Helping Uganda Schools", to meet the needs of some of the many young people in this part of Uganda who have difficulty learning. And the parade is a celebration, and an affirmation, of the rights of the disabled. For Sr Theresa's vision is to provide education for the children she witnessed as a teacher herself: children unable to access school at all, children struggling in the school system: ignored or worse, beaten, for not learning quickly enough, children missing out, through no fault of their own.

The band gather to lead the march

So, how did Sr Theresa come to be marching through Fort Portal on that December day? In answer, I shall attempt, here, to recount how the building of the

14

Good Shepherd School was achieved, and how Theresa's dream assumed reality; but additionally, I will also outline where the project has reached today, and what the vision for its future, and its future needs, may be. And I shall begin at the very beginning.

Chapter 1

Sister Theresa Abigaba

Born at the beginning of the 1960s, Sr. Theresa began life in the village of Kigarama, some six or seven kilometres outside Fort Portal, the sixth of nine children, her father a guard at the palace of the King of Toro. While her friends grew up and dreamed of men and marriage and children, the little Theresa wanted always only to be a nun. Her mother, she told me, was a devout Catholic, but it was her older sister who was sent, with carefully saved money, to see the Sisters in Kampala on Ugandan Martyr's day, (and who came back with saucy tales and eyes only for the dashing young priests.) But Theresa was single-minded, and got her wish. After completing her education up to Primary 7, she joined the sisterhood and attended Maria Goretti High School next to the Virika Convent, in Fort Portal. She lived her adolescence through the turbulent years of Ugandan rule by the despot Idi Amin, and recalls the fears and privations of that time, though she prefers not to, rather preferring to celebrate the more recent progress and successes of her country and its leadership.

Theresa joined the order of Banyatereza Sisters, an order initially established by a French priest, and now with bases in Uganda, Kenya and Rwanda (the Order of St Therese of the Child Jesus), and nurtured within it, she went on to study at Kinyamasika College, and then for her Diploma at Kikoba National Teacher Training College. This was followed later by a BA in Educational Management and Religious Studies at the internationally lauded Makerere University in Kampala.

It was , however, in 2002, while teaching in St Peter's and St Paul's Primary School in Fort Portal, that Theresa began to contemplate the problems facing children with learning or physical difficulties. The introduction of free Universal Primary Education by the Ugandan Government in 1997, while very welcome , had brought with it its own challenges. The result had been large, rapidly expanding classes of children, with insufficient teachers, teaching in hastily constructed buildings. The legislation encouraged schools to include children who were different, particularly those who were orphaned or disabled, but the truth was that if you found it difficult to get to school or to move around the buildings, or if, in the classroom, you found it difficult to concentrate or to hear the teacher, or, indeed if you just found the work hard, you either chose not to go to school, or, if you did attend, you tried to remain inconspicuous at the back of the room, and out of trouble.

One particular child troubled Theresa. Thomas had learnt very little since starting at the school, and his speech was limited. He did not seem able to understand instructions, but he could copy letters and add and subtract if given individual attention. He loved the company of the other children and was always at the centre of any game of football. But he soon became frustrated when expected to work, and would quickly hit out at staff and children alike , so he was constantly in trouble. As a result he had taken to hiding in the bushes outside the classroom, watching his friends until they came out to play. Here was a child Theresa felt had potential; a child who clearly wanted to come to school, but whose needs were too great to be met in a class of forty with only one teacher.

So Theresa began to develop the idea of starting her own school for children who found learning a challenge like this. She wanted the pupils to be valued for themselves and to be encouraged to fulfil their own potential, whatever that might be. However, the concept of "special" education such as we are used to in the developed world, was very new to Uganda, and there were no prototypes for Theresa to model her ideas upon; nevertheless, she was determined not to be put off. And determination is something Theresa has never been short of!

Chapter 2.
Fort Portal

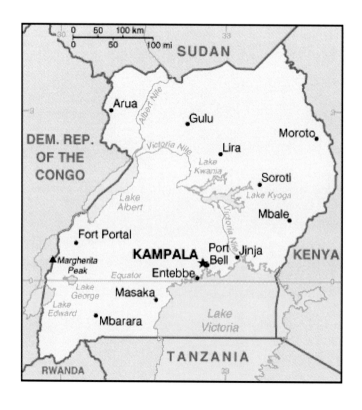

Fort Portal is not a big place. The population in the whole of the Kabarole District, of which it is the focus, is only some 400,000, spread out across an area about the size of Wales, largely rural and forested and with a high proportion of children and young people. Families live in villages, well off the beaten murrum red dust track, farming the land for their own consumption. Their staple diet consists of green bananas called matoke, usually cooked as a mash, and they keep goats and chickens. In the foothills of the beautiful Rwenzori mountains the rainfall is more reliable than in other areas of Uganda, and generally, the land is green and fertile, but there is still poverty and malaria; mothers still die and children are still damaged in childbirth; and safe water is still not available for many. However, some things are the same the world over: mobile phones are everywhere, internet cafe's abound, hydro-electric power (perhaps sometimes a little erratically) feeds the towns, and the progress of Manchester United, Arsenal, and Chelsea are followed obsessively. The trip to the Ugandan capital, Kampala, takes some five to six hours on one of the many crowded buses or the mini-bus taxis that travel the journey daily, and along the road is the evidence of earlier outsider influence, in vast tea plantations. Growing for export and for business is as yet in its early days, but lorries carry green bananas and pineapples to the city.

Green bananas are carried by bicycle to the main road

The local language is Rutoro, and the second language English, or less commonly, Swahili. Children pick up a smattering of English from early on, and any white visitor..."mzungu", (and there are still sufficiently few of them in number here for them to be a curiosity) is assailed with sing-song calls of: "Hello. How are you?"... "I am well, thankyou," from small smiling faces.

Everyone in Fort Portal, I find, is most welcoming, and, despite their limited resources, people are very generous. In the market fruit and vegetables are sold by volume, piled up into pyramids, rather than by weight, and a few extra are always thrown in to a purchase for good measure.

Vegetables in Mpanga market

Children walk to school, and can be seen along the roadsides on their way in the morning, sometimes covering several miles a day, and sometimes even barefoot, but always in uniform; or they live in, sleeping in cramped dormitories as boarders; or they travel to school by boda-boda (pillion on a motor cycle taxi). Education, though nominally free, carries with it the cost of the uniform (all school children wear a uniform), materials such as pencils and exercise books, toilet rolls, and sometimes other school overheads. With very limited income and often five or six children, parents are inevitably forced to make difficult decisions about who goes to school and for how long.

A boda-boda with passengers

Sadly, then, children whose potential for learning is impaired do not represent a good investment to their parents, and so they often miss out on education; they may even be seen as a burden to their families. That is not to say that their parents don't care about them, and, like parents the world over, they worry about them and about their future.

Chapter 3.
A Trip to the UK

"In a strange country you made me at home.

Seeking employment you found me a job,

Searching for kindness you held out your hand,

Now enter into the home of my Father."

Mother Teresa of Kolkata (from Matthew 25: 31-46)

It was in September 2003 that Sr Theresa first left Uganda to come to the UK. She had never been out of Africa…and she'd never seen an escalator! So arrival at a UK airport was a little daunting. Her fellow Sisters had put her forward for further education, and the Virika congregation had paid the fees for her to study for an MA in Educational Leadership and School Improvement at Manchester University. She followed this with a Diploma in Special Education, so was to be in the UK for four years. She arrived in her veil with £50 in her pocket for her living expenses. And Manchester was cold!

She was assigned a room in a student hall of residence in South Manchester, and began to explore the city's transport system. (She was to become an expert on Manchester buses, putting many a long-term Manchester resident to shame.) But it soon became clear that her £50 was not going to go far, and she was going to have to find a way of earning some money. And here begins a tale of acts of generosity, small kindnesses, and big commitments: pieces of a jigsaw that, fitted together, eventually led to the laying of the foundations of the Good Shepherd School.

It would be difficult to do justice to all those that contributed to this jigsaw, but perhaps we should start with Fr Albert. Fr Albert Byaruhanga hailed from Fort Portal. A genial erudite man who enjoyed a glass of wine and a good meal, particularly of Chinese cuisine, he had risen through the ranks of the Catholic hierarchy in Uganda, to have significant influence in the world of education. He was well travelled and worldly wise, and he knew that Theresa would find living in the UK a challenge. So, when he journeyed to an ecclesiastical conference in Dublin, he was delighted to meet Pawlik, who had been delegated to attend the same conference as the lay representative of his church just north of Manchester. Originally from Poland himself, but now long settled in the UK, Pawlik had experience of being the outsider, and he listened to Fr Albert's concerns about Theresa. On returning home he sought Theresa out in her college "digs" and welcomed her into his family.

Fr Albert was to go on to give more support to Theresa, and to welcome Western visitors, come to Uganda to help the school, into his home in Kampala. I, myself, benefitted from this hospitality on my first trip to Uganda, and have fond memories of his home among the jacaranda trees, where I was invited to acclimatise after my air flight before travelling to Fort Portal. Sadly, however, he was not to live long enough to see the children march through his home town. Fr Albert died in a road traffic accident on his way back to Fort Portal in October 2009.

Pawlik, though, proved himself a star. Not only did he invite Theresa to his home, but he introduced her to the matron of his local catholic home for the elderly....and here she was given her first job as a care assistant. And Theresa needed that: the Manchester climate did not suit her and she was cold. With her £50 she had explored the Manchester shops for a coat, and was horrified by the prices. It took her gradually growing circle of friends to suggest she try Primark...a recommendation that still today Theresa remembers with a smile, though later, as she grew to know Manchester better, she also discovered the bargains that could be had in the Charity shops and in Longsight Market.

But Theresa needed more permanent employment to pay her living expenses while she studied at the university. So she was advised to visit the Job Centre. When her turn came to be seen, she found herself explaining her problems to a small dark-haired lady with a warm and sympathetic Mancunian smile, called Marian. The lives of Marian and her family were to become very closely entwined with Theresa's, and this meeting was the start of a friendship that would blossom and deepen over the years; but it began with some very practical advice and help finding jobs...jobs in care homes, schools and hospitals all over the city...and a twenty pound note slipped into a handshake at the end.

Theresa, then, pursued her studies diligently, and, in her habit, travelled by bus to clean and care, and earn the money for her keep. But, of course, she didn't forget her calling, and one Sunday she attended an ecumenical service at St Augustine's Church at the end of which the Bishop of Salford drew her to one side. Bishop Brain was interested in her story: where she came from, what she was doing in England, her Order, and how she was coping so far from home. He invited her to Salford cathedral a few days later and introduced her to Sister Maureen Farrell, who worked for Manchester University and was well known for befriending foreign students. Sr Maureen became Theresa's guide and mentor, and it was to her that Theresa first confided her dream...the dream of founding a special school in an area of Africa where few such schools existed.

Theresa with Sr Maureen

Christmas, of course, is a special time for families, and so it happened that Sr Maureen took Theresa to a Yuletide party hosted by her nephew, Luke, and his wife, Diana, in their home in South Manchester. Here, by an open fire and a twinkling Christmas tree, Theresa was asked about her home, her studies and her plans. How different it all was: the cold, the dark evenings, and the bare trees of the English winter, from the heat, the constant twelve hour days, and the green banana groves of equatorial Fort Portal. But, encouraged by Sr Maureen, Theresa told Luke about the school she wanted to build, and how she needed a sponsor to get the project under way. A telephone call followed, and Luke relayed this conversation to Peter Mount, Chair of the Central Manchester Hospitals Trust, knowing that he had an interest in schools in Uganda. Peter Mount had, indeed, set up a registered charity: Helping Uganda Schools, which was already supporting the development of schools in Uganda, and particularly one specific school: St Zoe's in Mubende, half way between Kampala and Fort Portal. Peter Mount invited Theresa to come and see him, and offered her his support, with conditions...that the school be built to a high specification and that it demonstrate the best standards of education. These were challenges that Theresa was very willing to accept.

Theresa completed her studies in 2007. After returning to Uganda, however, she maintained her links with the UK, and, indeed, these have grown and strengthened. Theresa has come back on a number of occasions to visit her friends around Manchester, to report back on progress, and also to seek out new ideas and examples of good practice to take back to Fort Portal. Many have helped here, but perhaps three schools particularly warrant mention: Beckfoot School in

Bradford, Greenfold School (now part of the Orchards federation) in Bolton, and St John Vianney School in Stretford, all of whose staff and pupils have been particularly generous with their time, their hospitality, their expertise, and their fund-raising. Yet other schools have hosted visits from Theresa, and raised money for her venture, and if she has learnt from them , they have also learnt from her...about a country, much the same size as the UK, but very different from the impression of Africa of famine, war and drought so often given by the media, where children go to school to learn the same things as they do here, where they like to play football and ride bicycles, and also, of course, from where this year's Olympic Marathon winner came. And, naturally, Theresa's visits, as well, have had to include some special experiences to recall back in Uganda, not least... a trip to the Theatre of Dreams, and a sighting of Wayne Rooney's shirt!

Even nuns can have heroes

Chapter 4

Laying the Foundations

In 2007 Theresa returned to Fort Portal and, with the support and blessing of her Order, and particularly her Mother Superior, she set about looking for a plot of land on which to build her school. With the help of HUGS (the charity, Helping Uganda Schools) five acres of land were purchased about 5Km outside Fort Portal just off the road that leads south-east to Ndali and some of the most beautiful of the Crater Lakes.

One of the Crater Lakes outside Fort Portal

These bottomless, blue, steep sided lakes, the water filled craters of extinct volcanoes, and the moonscape-like cones around them, are a reminder of the proximity of the Rift Valley and of the local earthquake potential. Only a few years previously the Virika Cathedral in Fort Portal had been destroyed by an earthquake and rebuilt to specifications incorporating 'quake resistant technology. A local architect, therefore, was sought who would take a similar approach to the building of the school. By February 2008 the foundations had been laid for the first classrooms.

Laying the foundations for the first classrooms

The building site was on a hill with the land sloping down to a small stream along the perimeter. The first structure was to be at the top of the hill and was to comprise six classrooms with a central office and store area, arranged along a connecting, open, roofed veranda. From here there were breathtaking views across the undulating plain: a patchwork of grazing land, banana plantations and cultivated fields.

The view from the first classrooms

The construction work itself was highly labour intensive, massive rocks used in the foundations being man-handled into place on wheelbarrows, and water for cement brought up from the stream in jerry cans. Lunch, matoke, was cooked on site by the workers themselves. Whenever possible Theresa drew her workforce from the local community and sourced her materials from nearby, though she was at pains to ensure that the bricks and mortar etc. were of a good standard, which sometimes meant casting further afield for suitable suppliers. Nevertheless, while the focus was on quality, there was, undoubtedly, a carefully managed spin off for the local economy. From the start then, this special school would be special to its own community.

Building the school

Slowly, slowly the walls began to grow, and the school took shape. A corrugated iron roof was added...effective at keeping the children dry and cool, but deafening during the storms of the rainy season; and water butts were installed to collect the rain. The inner walls were plastered (a feature often missing in Ugandan schools) and the outer walls painted in bright, welcoming, and business like colours.

Completing the first classrooms

By August 2008 the school was ready to open its doors to its first pupils, and Theresa had recruited a Management Committee to oversee her work, drawn from her Church and the local business, political and academic community. Although the school was to welcome children from families of all faiths or of none, she had always known that the school should be named

"The Good Shepherd School", but now she had to appoint teachers and decide which children to admit.

Chapter 5

Assessing the Need

In 2008, while the foundations for the first classrooms of the Good Shepherd School were being laid, Sr Theresa and I, a retired British paediatrician, made an attempt to find out how many children there might be in the villages around Fort Portal, who had disabilities or learning difficulties, and what their needs were. While we expected that there would be a lot of children hidden out there, there is very little available information about children who have special needs, and how they live, either in Uganda or much of the rest of Africa, so we were prepared for anything. Nevertheless, we were somewhat overwhelmed by the numbers brought to our "clinics" by desperate parents, and also by the severity of some of the children's difficulties.

Thirteen sites were chosen for these "clinic" sessions, and parents were invited by word of mouth to bring their children. Each day we arrived to find many, many children waiting with their parents to be seen, sitting patiently on benches or on the ground under the trees, all day if necessary. I was always offered a drink and biscuits or a banana, and there was always a plastic bowl, a jug of water, and a bar of soap with which I could wash my hands, but the parents seemed to bring no food or drink, and I worried at how stoically they waited. One mother waited like this with her little girl, Mary, on her knee, taking her out when need be, for, like all babies here, she had no nappy, until her turn finally came. Beneath the white lace and satin dress her mother had clearly dressed her in specially for the occasion, I found all the tell tale signs of the progressive muscle disorder that would inevitably take her life in the not too distant future. Although I hoped it had been made clear that we were "fact finding" for the establishment of a school, it was difficult not to feel desperately sad and guilty that we had nothing to offer a child like this. Maybe very little could have been done for Mary, and certainly her life could not have been prolonged by Western medicine, but I could not help but reflect on the support and advice that her mother would have received, at the very least, in the UK. Struggling with the language, Theresa translating between Rutoro and English, we did our best to give explanations and simple advice in response to her questions, only to feel even more guilty at her gratitude. This was not to be the only time I struggled with the ethics of what we were doing. Or questioned whether the Western way of doing things...here researching the evidence base, (and raising hopes,) before meeting the need...was applicable to the resource poor setting of Africa.

The children were seen in churches, in school rooms, in dispensaries....wherever there was a room. And together, Theresa and I met between four and five hundred young people with learning difficulty or disability, though more turned up with other health problems, particularly severe conjunctivitis caused by the ubiquitous red dust. (And it was difficult to deny that these children, too, were in fact disabled in school by their red and itching eyes.) As the terminology for disability is limited in the local dialect, the message reaching the villages was sometimes misinterpreted, and on one occasion we turned up to be faced with an enormous group of over a hundred children orphaned by AIDS. Our remit would have been totally unmanageable had we included these socially disadvantaged children as well as the children with definable disability, but it was hard turning them away.

The problem, we found, was much greater even than we expected: a challenge for the school to meet just a tiny proportion of the need. But what kept us going was the thought that aiming at the tip of this iceberg of need (or more appropriately for Uganda: the ears of this hippopotamus) Sr Theresa might kindle a beacon that would light the way for others.

Many of the children we saw were "slow learners", like John and Matthew, who turned up in their Sunday best suits. Their parents often described these children as suffering from "mental confusion", and they worried that they were very vulnerable, and that without employment they would end up abused or as beggars.

John and Matthew wait their turn to be seen

Others had physical difficulties such as cerebral palsy affecting one or all of their limbs. One young man, Samuel, who could not stand, and whose knees and hips were bent beneath him, fixed by muscle contractures, indicated how he helped in his father's shop. He had been born early, and his parents had not expected him to live, but he had survived, and with good humour. He was brought by his father, a weather-beaten old man who ran a small roadside "lock-up" shop selling everything from batteries to avocados. His son resembled a little stick man, his skinny body distorted by his stiff limbs, and, though he told us he was 15, his father easily carried him in his arms. He showed us that he could count, though he could not read or write, and yet he was clearly proud of his role: taking the money from the customers for his father in his shop, and he enjoyed telling us about it. And another young lady, Sharon, laughed at me when I asked her how she got there to see us, as she came alone. With delight she demonstrated how, despite arms and legs that refused to do what she wanted, she could ride a boda-boda. Her limbs and her speech were severely affected by spasms and involuntary movements, and it was difficult to understand her, but her spirit was indomitable. Neither of these young people had been able to attend school, though they both clearly had considerable potential.

Nearly a quarter of the children were deaf, with little or no hearing and no speech, though they often communicated quite effectively using sophisticated gesture or simple signs. If they went to school at all they were generally surprisingly well socially integrated: perhaps there was a lesson to be learnt here for us in the West. But academically they were limited to copying exercises from the blackboard with little or no understanding of their meaning. Sometimes they came with deaf parents, but often the cause of their hearing loss was unclear. None had hearing aids.

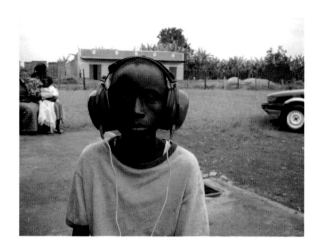

A hearing test in the open air

Yet others had epilepsy, doubly disabled by uncontrolled seizures, and by societal attitudes to their supposed "possession" by demons. Sometimes these children were receiving inadequate or inappropriate treatment for their convulsions, but often their parents were unable to afford the few shillings needed for their tablets, or they had stopped giving the medication to their children because it had failed to "cure" them, not understanding the long term nature of the condition and its treatment. Often these children bore the scars of severe burns from falling on to open fires during a seizure.

But saddest of all were the little ones whose learning and physical difficulties were most profound, for without help they appeared destined to become increasingly handicapped and to be limited to lying immobile on a makeshift bed. Without advice on positioning and muscle stretches they were already developing fixed joints and were proving difficult to feed, and , although one might have expected their early demise as a result, we saw plenty of older children like this , usually severely undernourished but nevertheless otherwise well cared for, who had survived, but only with a very reduced quality of life.

And what was the cause of the children's difficulties?...it was hard to say, particularly in view of the problems I had with the language and its translation, but birth injury, accident, illness, and genetic predisposition all seemed to play a part. We often heard a tale of a precipitating episode of severe (cerebral) malaria, but evidence of damage from polio or measles was rare, testifying to the hard work of the local immunisers. Some disability was clearly preventable if the underlying condition could have been treated appropriately, like the toddlers we saw with "club feet", who needed only minor orthopaedic intervention. But more significantly, many of the children were handicapped more by the "knock-on" effects of their impairment than by the impairment itself, as it prevented them from accessing opportunities, such as education, which might have enabled them to reach their full potential.

When we had finally completed our village visits, Theresa and I sat down to consider what the information we had gathered meant for the development of the school. Struggling with intermittent access to "dial-up" internet services, we searched for similar experience to ours, and for expertise adapted to the African environment. While other projects and schools for disabled children existed, they were widely scattered, often run by Westerners, and rarely as forward thinking as Theresa's ideas. It was difficult to escape the conclusion that Theresa was very much on her own with her vision.

Chapter 6

The First Children

So where do you start, faced with such enormous need? Well, Theresa started by quietly opening the doors of her school to twenty eight learning disabled children in August 2008, and, by February 2009, she had thirty five children on roll. Existing schools for children with disabilities in Uganda are largely residential, and sited in centres such as Mbarara or Kampala, doing nothing to help the understanding and acceptance of such children by their own communities. In Fort Portal the only educational provision specifically for children with disabilities was the small "demonstration" unit attached to the local teacher training college, also entirely residential. The Good Shepherd School was therefore breaking new ground: none of the children were to live in. That brought with it its own problems, and limited the intake to those living close by , or whose parents could afford or could organise a means of travel every day.

Lessons outside...the early days

Furthermore, the school was neither Government funded nor a charity per se, and there were considerations of sustainability to address. Thus, though low, school fees were charged, and the children were expected to wear a uniform. Parents, then, expected outcomes.

Of the first children admitted, two thirds had relatively mild learning difficulties. Such children would have easily been accommodated in mainstream classes in the UK, where there are high staffing levels and differentiated curricula, but it is easy to see how much more handicapped they might be in a Ugandan setting. However, they had potential that could be nurtured in small classes with more individualised help. It would be possible, therefore, to show results.

Inevitably then, the first children were, to some extent, "self-selected" and generally quite able, though they did include two children who were profoundly hearing impaired, several with physical disabilities, and a few with more severe learning difficulties. As one might expect of such a self-selected, and well motivated intake, the children appeared adequately nourished and healthy. I have visited the school every February since 2008 carrying out health checks on the children, weighing and measuring them, and testing their vision and hearing. Parasitic infestations are very common in children in this part of the world and often cause anaemia, but, when we checked this, very few of the pupils were significantly anaemic,(though we did treat them all for infections such as hookworm just in case.)

One of the first children to start in the Nursery Class was Asumpta. Born with a spinal abnormality that caused her back to curve and that affected the nerves to one of her legs, Asumpta was only able to shuffle across the floor. Her affected leg was paralysed and fixed in a forever "cross-legged" position, and , though an active contributor to classroom activities, she had to be carried to the latrine, to the boda-boda at home time, or to be included in the other children's play. It was heartbreaking to see her sitting at her purpose made wooden desk, or on the teacher's lap, clapping hands, joining in the singing, and swaying to the rhythm of the drums at "song-time", but unable to join in the other children's dancing.

She lived with her mother and her older brother, Ronald, in a nearby village, in a little house with concrete walls, a dirt floor, and a tin roof, without running water or electricity. Her mother cooked on an open fire at the back, and struggled to make ends meet, though, like her daughter, she always had a ready smile and an offer of hospitality for a visitor. When Asumpta had been born she had been assessed by the local doctors, but the cost of the investigations and of the surgery suggested was prohibitive, not least because it included the cost of travel to Kampala, to Mulago, the University Hospital, and living expenses whilst there .

Knowing that Asumpta's future depended upon her ability to live independently, the school raised sponsorship to send her to the Katalemwa Hospital in Kampala. Katalemwa and the CORSU Hospital, where Asumpta had much of her surgery, are run by charities, and treatment is largely free, or at least at minimal cost. However, for Asumpta and her mother, there were costs for travel, food, and accommodation, and for aids such as crutches, medicines, and investigations like X-rays, and the treatment itself was long drawn out. Asumpta underwent a series of operations over more than two years, first to release her leg from its tethered position, and then to straighten it using a metal cage to slowly rotate the bones. However, the first step was to provide her with crutches, to which she took like a duck to water...freedom at last! Subsequently she has been able to abandon the crutches and, with a built up shoe, she is able to dance and play football with her friends. This is unlikely to be the end of her mobility problems, and she will probably need more crutches, at the very least, in the future, but for now she can rejoice in wearing shoes and being like the other girls. Though her agility may be more limited again in the future, her difficulties should not stop her now from making an active contribution to her community. And, of course, though her experience of hospitals and doctors has made her more wary of adults (particularly white ones), she is also more worldly wise and confident, and she has grown quite bossy...perhaps a leader of men in the making?

Asumpta's first days in school

First steps

Asumpta joins in the dancing

and the

football

Of course, news of the school spread and parents sought it out for their children, so pupil numbers began to rise...hence there were eighty children in school at the end of the Good Shepherd's first full academic year. These were the children marching through Fort Portal on that special day in December 2009, down the dusty main road, past the Rwenzori Travellers Inn, where the guests watched from the balcony with their Cokes and their Nile beers, past the Total garage, where the private-hire taxis fill up with just enough petrol to take their next fare, past the headquarters of the Voice of Toro radio station, past Andrew's supermarket, past the bank, and the mosque, and down the hill to the Buhiinga Government Referral Hospital, where they were picked up and taken back to school. This road is very straight, and from outside the Standbic Bank you can see from the beginning of their walk to the end: a distance of some mile and a half. It took them three long hours.

Chapter 7

Roots and Branches: the Growth of the School

One of the most severely disabled children to start at the school at the very beginning was a young woman, Christine, seventeen years old, with Down Syndrome, whose ability to learn was very limited. She was a delightful young lady, who, nevertheless, was very willing and eager to do what she could. She reinforced for Theresa the need to provide some form of vocational training for the older children, that would enable them to earn, for themselves, a simple living in the fullness of time. For, although the school had started essentially as a primary school, the ages of the children stretched much further. From the start, then, it was often possible to see a group of girls sitting on the floor in the office area, crocheting and weaving baskets.

After the first foundations were laid the school grew and developed rapidly. Buildings were added, including another block of classrooms, within which there was a large area designated for vocational training, and a school hall. This dedicated vocational classroom now houses sewing machines and knitting machines, and there is also an outside sheltered carpentry workshop.

Young people now have light and space within which to learn a craft.

The new classrooms have ensured that the school is able to offer a full curriculum for children from classes Primary 1 to Primary 7, and a new latrine block has been constructed to meet the needs of the growing numbers of pupils. Sr Theresa has been able to move from the Virika Convent to purpose built accommodation on site, where she has been joined by two other sisters:

(another) Sr Theresa, who teaches religious studies and vocational skills, and the young Sr Domitilla, who is herself training to be a teacher. The Sisters are also able to offer accommodation to two paying guests at a time in their home within the school grounds.

The school in 2012

A dedicated team of teachers has been recruited, with leadership from Friday John, the Deputy Head. They include the delightful nursery teacher, Agnes, a virtuoso on the African drums, and Junior, himself severely hearing impaired, who teaches the children to sign. Being deafened after he learnt to speak and not deaf from birth, Junior has good spoken language, though he has a hearing aid (provided many years ago by well meaning visitors) which has sadly proven exceedingly difficult to service.

Some of the school staff: Friday John second from left back row, Agnes second from left front row

The teachers are very welcoming and very committed to the children, and all live locally. It is in the nature of such a new service, provided for a previously ignored group of children, however, that experience working with such children with special needs is very limited in the area. Teaching in Uganda tends to be very didactic, and, of necessity, with one teacher sometimes to classes of ninety or more, subject focussed rather than child focussed. The idea of differentiating the curriculum to meet the needs of individual children is a strange one here, and there is little understanding of how to address problem behaviours in children who challenge their teachers because of social or communication difficulties. Sr Theresa has taken ideas back with her from the UK about special needs education, but Western ideas are not always transferrable to such a different environment and culture.

The school, however, has grasped this nettle, and has undertaken a number of exciting in service training projects. Hannah, a VSO volunteer working at the local teacher training college was asked to lead a workshop on child centred learning, and, drawing on expertise from the deaf community in Uganda , sign language training for all the staff has been organised. Friday John has himself, in his own time, attended post-graduate training in special needs education at Kyambogo College in Kampala.

But still the school could only meet the needs of a very limited group of children and Theresa was regularly being approached by parents of more severely disabled children for help: children with autism, children with profound learning difficulties, children who could not walk or care for themselves at all, children, indeed, for whom the march through Fort Portal would have been impossible, but for whom it was also a rallying cry. The barriers seemed insurmountable…where was the expertise to come from to help these little ones? And how could they be reached in their villages?

Step one was to provide the school with a means of transport. Once again, British donors dug deep into their pockets or committed themselves to sponsored challenges to raise the cost. Hills were climbed and miles walked or run, and one donor even scaled Mt Kilimanjaro. Eventually enough money was raised and a reconditioned cabin truck was purchased, (and blessed), and a driver hired. This, it must be acknowledged, was an expensive investment, as vehicles, spare parts, insurance, and particularly petrol, transported by road across Kenya from the coast, are all extremely costly.

Blessing the new truck

Nevertheless, by 2011, Sr Theresa was ready to take the next step in the development of her vision. Since 2008 her links with services for children with special needs in the North West of England had grown and strengthened. While on visits here she had met and observed many health and educational professionals working with children with all sorts of difficulties. She was finally able to persuade four of them to come out to Uganda to help her start her "Outreach Project" for a small group of more severely disabled children. Emma, a physiotherapist, Eric, an educational psychologist, Dan, a paediatrician, and Helen, a specialist paediatric nurse, travelled to Uganda in February 2012, to work for two weeks with me and the school staff, including a newly appointed teacher, Margret, recruited specially for the purpose, to set up what might more accurately be called an "Inreach Project".

The four, well briefed but with no previous experience of Africa, arrived in Entebbe in the black of night, their hearts in their mouths, their malaria prophylaxis in their pockets, and their ears ringing with advice on how to survive the tropics. They spent their first night in a convent, sleeping under mosquito nets, washing in large plastic washing up bowls with hot water provided in jerry cans, and gingerly tasting their first Ugandan food. The following day the cabin truck took them to Fort Portal. Here they based themselves in the Rwenzori View Guesthouse, where they celebrated a 50th birthday, Valentine's Day, and Mardi Gras in style, hosted by Ineke Jongerius, the proprietor. Ineke, originally from the Netherlands herself, invites her guests to share their meals around a single table, so they were also treated to a succession of travellers' tales from all over the globe...indeed it sometimes seemed as if the whole world and his wife were passing through Fort Portal, exploring, holidaying, preaching, "giving something back", or just resting on their way to see the gorillas.

From the Rwenzori View the four travelled daily to the school. In a program that mirrored the first fact finding mission in 2008, parents were invited to bring their children to clinics, this time held at the school, so that their needs could be assessed and programs devised, with Margret, for their teaching and care. This time, though, the children were transported to the clinics in the school's vehicle.

Watching the Team from the UK work with the children prompted me to reflect upon my own career. When I started work with disabled children in hospital in the early 1970s in the UK many of the children had been permanently resident in long-stay institutions. It had not been uncommon for parents to be advised to place their "handicapped" children in such care and forget about them. However, within my professional lifetime we have come a long way: the long stay hospitals have been closed, and every child has an indisputable right to education... and increasingly inclusive education alongside their more "able" peers. I like to think we have learnt from this evolutionary process, and that it is only fair that we share some of the experience gained, with those starting out on the journey toward the establishment of services for disabled children and their families. I hope, then, that the work of the team, alongside the teachers in the school, is received as helpful and collaborative, and not as another manifestation of covert "colonialism".

In this spirit, through a process of assessment, advice and discussion, around twenty children were selected to take part in the "Outreach Project", including Simon and his cousin. Simon had been a healthy little boy until he was eight, and his mother proudly showed Margret a photo of him at a birthday party prior to his illness:

Then one day he had caught malaria.

The type of malaria prevalent in Uganda is particularly virulent, and children are very vulnerable. The importance of protection from mosquitoes, particularly at night when those that carry malaria bite, is not well understood. If you are immune to the bites themselves you don't feel the insects biting anyway so they are easy to ignore. Mosquito nets are hot to sleep under and not always available free, and to be effective they need to be undamaged and ideally treated with insecticide. So they don't get used, and as a result malaria is common. As children grow older they tend to develop some degree of immunity to the parasite, and bouts of infection tend to get less severe, but attacks in young children leave behind a trail of death and damage. And most severe are the bouts of cerebral malaria, when the brain is affected, and children, if they survive, may be left deaf, learning disabled or paralysed.

And this is what had happened to Simon... an episode of cerebral malaria. His ability to move had been most severely affected. He lost the ability to coordinate movements and his muscles became very stiff. He could no longer stand, or even sit, without help and support. His hands wouldn't open to take hold of anything, and his arms couldn't reach out. He could no longer feed himself or speak. He did, however, continue to have a winning smile, and it was clear he was intensely interested in what was happening around him. He was brought by his mother to be seen by "the team", who felt he would really enjoy coming to the school, even if it was only for one day a week. Here he could be offered physiotherapy: stretching exercises for his arms and legs that his mother could learn to do, a special seat so he could be upright to see what was happening around him, and the opportunity to make friends , interact and sing with other children. Then perhaps it would be possible to find ways to help him to communicate and begin to have some control over his world again. His mother was delighted.

Simon and his mum

Another Man U supporter!

So now, Simon is one of the small group of parents and children who are brought to the school, for one day each, each week, where, depending on the severity of their difficulties and their age, they may take part in a "Nurture Group", they may receive physiotherapy, or they may be taught simple crafts or life skills. A physiotherapist from the local Government Referral Hospital visits monthly and is extremely helpful in teaching parents and staff exercises for the children, and in seeking out wheelchairs and aids to help the children make the most of their own special skills, whatever these are.

The physiotherapist at work

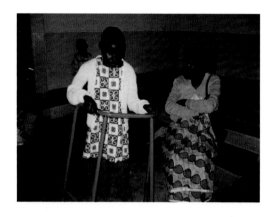

The school hall is used for the "Nurture Groups" of four or five children. Those that are not mobile are "treated" with exercises by the physiotherapist or their parents on plastic covered foam mattresses on the floor, and, while some toys have been acquired, more are invented using locally available materials, such as pebbles in clear plastic water bottles. A family member comes with each child, not always the mother, and teacher Margret leads group activities: singing, action rhymes and stories. The English visitors adapted, and, indeed, performed, "Old MacDonald's Farm" and "Ten Green Bottles", for the children, and these renditions were received with great enthusiasm, although their musicality, it has to be said, was surpassed by the singing and dancing that the children in the main school offered them in return at their farewell assembly.

The bazungus perform Ten Green Bottles

and the children reciprocate

In its first year the "Outreach Group" has bedded in to the school. It is now being supported by another UK Charity as well as "Helping Uganda Schools": "Improving Chances for Ugandan Mothers and Children", whose Chair of Trustees, Len Richards, and his wife, Jackie, have been to visit the project. Only one child has dropped out, and the parents are enthusiastic. The rest of the school thrives, and the children there are making progress. Visitors are met with an atmosphere of quiet industry and clearly happy pupils. The buildings look good, and now there are even roses growing in the garden, nurtured in front of the main buildings. Sr Theresa and her teachers are rightly proud of their achievements, and celebrated with their own triumphant "Olympic Games" for the children this year... the year the UK celebrated such a spectacular Paralympics... progress indeed for those original Fort Portal marchers!

The girls play volleyball

Chapter 8

Keeping Going

From the start, the issue of sustainability has been one that has challenged everyone: the school, Sr Theresa and her management committee, and many of her supporters. Providing a service to a marginalised section of the population does not immediately generate much revenue, while teachers still need to be paid regularly and the upkeep costs of buildings accrue. The school is run with the greatest economy, the little ones learning to write with chalk on slate, the older children copying their lessons from the blackboard into exercise books in pencil. While teaching resources such as textbooks and wall charts are few, what resources there are need to be bought and replenished.

The land on which the school is built is rich and fertile and every inch possible is cultivated...greens, carrots, potatoes (known here as "Irish" potatoes), tomatoes, beans, groundnuts, all grow prolifically, as well as green bananas... but none sufficiently to raise a realistic income for the school.

Tilling the soil in the school garden

The school keeps goats, and the children benefit from mid-day porridge made with goats milk. There are cows, and chickens, and pigs for fattening for sale (pork meat is prized here), and the stream has been diverted into ponds for breeding tilapia fish. But even this is not sufficient to underwrite the costs of the growing school project.

Early on Sr Theresa persuaded "Helping Uganda Schools" to buy her a "tipper truck" which she hires out to raise funds. This has been a success, though work for the truck, mainly transporting materials for the building trade , tends to be seasonal. Other ideas have been mooted, e.g. growing tea, running a mini-bus for hire, or keeping bees, but most require significant initial investment, both of money and expertise...not easily come by.

The school's tipper truck

Perhaps the greatest expenditure that needs ongoing financing is the transport. It is difficult to see how the school could continue, or even possibly expand, its work with the most severely disabled children without the cabin truck, its servicing and its fuel: costly basics we take for granted in the UK.

Similarly, all the children would benefit greatly from access to the kinds of information technology available to every child in the UK, but computers need power, and renewable energy requires initial investment, for example in photovoltaic cells (solar panels), and then in their maintenance. Though, of course, sunlight is easily and freely available, and the know-how to support the exploitation of solar energy does exist locally.

School fees are an obvious source of income, but if the school is to attract the most disabled children and begin to change attitudes toward disability, fees need to be kept low, and sometimes waived. Walking the very fine line between creating dependence and reaching the most needy is very difficult, both for the individual and the organisation. Dependence on Western "Aid" funding makes a project like the Good Shepherd School very vulnerable: charity monies may "dry up" at any time; and at the same time... do the ties that bind donor and recipient inhibit entrepreneurial risk taking?

Sustainability will continue to be a challenge for the Good Shepherd School for a long time yet.

Chapter 9

What does the Future Hold?

"the Ears of the Hippopotamus"

In five years Sr Theresa and the Good Shepherd School have travelled a long way. Some one hundred and fifty children are now benefitting from education who might not otherwise have done so. Some of these children have severe disabilities and the school is setting an example to the community around it of how such children, who may be seen as "different" or even feared, can be valued, and can contribute to society in their own way. Through events such as the march through the town, the school is engaging the local population in raising awareness of the rights of all disabled people. One father, whose child took part in the march in 2009, said that his daughter had been "useless and a waste of time. But now she has been at school she comes home so happy. She is able to do things around the house. She irons my clothes. She is a new person."

So where does the school go from here? The number of children whose needs are being addressed is still relatively small. Perhaps, however, in time, the "Outreach" will truly become outreach, taking support, information, and advice out to more parents and children where they live, in the villages, and out to other schools around the region. It would be good to see the school become a "Resource Hub" for these schools and communities.

Hopefully, the involved parents will be empowered by their and their children's experiences to join together to support each other and to support the school... possibly even developing into a forceful lobby for disability rights, and contributing, themselves, to the sustainability of the school. Ideally the school needs to find a way to address the health needs of the most marginalised children that it works with, and particularly those who suffer uncontrolled seizures because of inadequately treated epilepsy.

Maybe the school will grow, maybe it won't...... but, no doubt, so long as it survives, little by little it will change views, debunk myths and superstition, and dispel fear. Children challenged by learning difficulty, illness, or disability will then gradually cease to be secondarily handicapped by societal attitudes and actions.

And Sr Theresa will continue, no doubt, to develop and refine her vision.

And the ears of the hippopotamus?.........well, hippos lie in the river, their huge grey bodies and big flat heads beneath the water, with only their ears showing. Like the tip of an iceberg, the ears are the tip of a great submerged bulk . So, the Good Shepherd School has started to meet the needs of a tiny proportion of the children who need special help in school in Africa. We cannot forget all the others that seem invisible, submerged, hidden, out of sight, but Sr Theresa's dream is trail-blazing for them all, and, eventually, the hippopotamus will slowly but surely emerge from the water.

Epilogue

Afterthoughts

It would be easy to dismiss this story as a fairy tale of dreams come true... of African smiles and sunshine... of warm hearted generosity. But that would be to deny the underlying hard work, and, indeed, the tears, that have contributed to the evolution of Theresa's first ideas into the reality of the Good Shepherd School.

For there have been misunderstandings, cross-cultural confusions, and linguistic misinterpretations. Concentrated in one small project have been many of the concerns that exist about delivering aid to the developing world. Issues of ownership of the project (for at the end of the day this must be Theresa's project and not that of the Western donors,) have been set against the need to assure donors of the proper use of their money, when Western perspectives can be so different to those so far away. The spectre of "aid dependency" has haunted many transactions, and hence provoked the anxieties about sustainability. Fear of corruption has raised its ugly head, as it always does in Africa. But, in parenthesis, when does help and advice become disguised colonialism? Other concerns simmer beneath the surface…what should or should not be the role of the Church or the State in the development of schools such as this? What "Western" practices and expectations are culturally appropriate or sustainable on the other side of the world? And what practices, particularly childcare practices, culturally acceptable in Africa but perhaps not condoned in the UK, should be addressed or can be assimilated within the process of development and change?

I have even been asked directly how such expenditure of resource and expertise as HUGS and "Improving Chances" have invested in such a small project can be justified in an area where there is such a shortage of the most basic health care... but then: "A society that treats its most vulnerable members with compassion is a more just and caring society for all" (World Health Organisation 2002.)

I offer no answers to the questions raised by these afterthoughts, I simply offer you this narrative. I hope you have enjoyed reading it. If you have supported HUGS or "Improving Chances" in the past... thankyou. If you are considering supporting us now ... please do. Remember the children who marched through Fort Portal on that December day in 2009 with their posters: "Disability is not Inability... Every Child has a Right to Education." They are still there... and you can make them smile!